ISBN 978-0-259-44291-2
PIBN 10817308

English
Français
Deutsche
Italiano
Español
Português

www.forgottenbooks.com

Mythology Photography **Fiction**
Fishing Christianity **Art** Cooking
Essays Buddhism Freemasonry
Medicine **Biology** Music **Ancient
Egypt** Evolution Carpentry Physics
Dance Geology **Mathematics** Fitness
Shakespeare **Folklore** Yoga Marketing
Confidence Immortality Biographies
Poetry **Psychology** Witchcraft
Electronics Chemistry History **Law**
Accounting **Philosophy** Anthropology
Alchemy Drama Quantum Mechanics
Atheism Sexual Health **Ancient History**
Entrepreneurship Languages Sport
Paleontology Needlework Islam
Metaphysics Investment Archaeology
Parenting Statistics Criminology
Motivational

THE TRIUMPH OF TRUTH,

—OR—

Science, Philosophy & Religion

Extract from a Work on the Philosophy of Life,

BY

R. M. GOODMAN,

MARIETTA, GA.

4 6

Entered according to Act of Congress by R. M. GOODMAN, 1883, in the Office of
the Librarian of Congress, at Washington, D.C.

ATLANTA, GEORGIA,
W. T. CHRISTOPHER & BROTHER, PRINTERS
69½ Whitehall Street,
1883.

PREFACE.

THE following problem made a lasting impression on the mind of the writer at an early age :

> "We are born, we laugh, we weep,
> We mourn, we droop, we die.
> Alas! whv do we laugh, and weep?
> WHY do we droop and die?
> Who can solve this problem great?
> Alas! not I."

FAITH and the Imagination are antagonists unequal to the march of appaling FACTS. In the arena of Intelect knowledge must be met with knowledge, or, Theology can never solve the problem.

In vain did the writer of the book of Job essay to do this. Equally in vain the earnest Wolaston, the writers of the Bridgewater books, the learned Paley, and many others, attempted the solution of the problem, and with all the light derived from the study of Nature cast upon it, from the twilight of Egyptian history to the present day, the problem remains unsolved.

Beautiful is the story of Gautama. Heir-apparent to an empire, with youth, power, honor, affluence, a lovely wife and child—if the gratification of the senses could bring contentment, he should have been happy. But, of all his countrymen, having no ills of their own, he was most miserable. Contemplating the brevity of life, the depravity of animal indulgence, sickness, sorrow, pain and death, incident to mortality, his soul revolted at the apparently purposeless and irrational order of nature. Moved by pity, commiseration, benevolence, in vain they attempted to prevent his escape to the meditations of solitude, where he hoped to be enlightened. In the dead hours of night he abandoned all—

> "Speak low," he said, "and bring my horse,
> For now the hour is come when I must quit
> This golden prison, where my heart lives caged,
> To find the *truth*, which henceforth I will seek
> For all men's sake, until the truth be found."

In a hermit's cell, living upon charity, for years his mind wrestled with the terrible enigma of Good and Evil. After deep study of Nature and its laws, he found enough of the Truth, in the discovery of the law of progressive development to satisfy the emotions and Intellect of the Soul. Then, he conceived, that by the subordination of animal selfishness to virtue—to love, charity, and w sdom, even here the soul could be brought in harmony with Nature and sure to reach Nirvana, the state of the blest.*

The story is beautiful, and given to the world 500 years

---

*See a work recently issued by the Standard Publishing House, N. Y., entitled "Errors Chains," a work of profound research in the history of Religion.

B. C., it is not wonderful that it gives inspiration to-day to nearly one-half of the human race.

But, he did not solve the problem. That solution can only come from the discovery of the cause of the law of Progressive Development. If that cause is matter, then Nirvana means Rest—the extinction of life—the annihilation of the Soul. If that cause is mind, then it means, for the Soul, infinite life and immortal happiness. So the old problem, of all ages, and all climes, viewed from the light of nature, remains as from the beginning.

The issue is between DEISM and MATERIALISM--an issue resulting solely from the absence of FACTS, on both sides, which it is the object of these pages to present in their proper connection, that Science, Philosophy and Religion may be exhibited in harmony with each other and MUTUALLY illustrative of the solution of the above problem, and the WISDOM, the POWER and the GOODNESS of GOD.

In 1860, memorable in our country as the opening of the Great Rebellion, precipitated upon us in the face of the solemn warnings of Washington, by aggressions of a faction at the North, enacting evil that good might come, and the dominant faction in the South, maddened by these aggressions, the writer employed himself in supervising the printing of a little work he had written, entitled "THE PHILOSOPHY OF LIFE." The page following on "INSPIRATION," is copied from that work without alteration. It was truth THEN, it is truth NOW and will be truth FOREVER.

Recent advances in Materialism—in Atheism—have prompted the succeeding elaboration of the part of the original Essay on Science, Philosophy and Religion.

With little aid from art and within a compass so narrow as this brief essay the light of human knowledge may not be concentrated upon the exposition of the great Truth so as to bring it clearly and indubitably to the mind. But if it has reached the point of discovery of the Astronomer, who, observing the purturbations of one of our solar planets, conceived, not only a cause, but the cause, and indicated the direction in the Heavens where that cause would be found and was found ; so, if these pages are only suggestive to some more fortunate mind, the end will be attained in the triumph of Truth.

If the work should be regarded by any one worthy of comment, the writer will please have the remarks mailed to my address.

INSPIRATION.

All TRUTH, whether intuitive or demonstrative; whether evolved from the native vigor of the mind, or, resulting from cultivated intellect; whether laboriously discovered in exploring the principles of matter or mind, or found in the contemplation of the Attributes of God—is Inspiration and comes from God.* Galilleo—Columbus—Newton, were inspired with great truths. It was Inspiration which enabled SOCRATES to teach his friends a just conception of God—PLATO to say that the Soul emanated from God—and JESUS to teach us, that GOD is our FATHER, a name dear to the human heart, expressive at once of Origin, and Love UNBOUNDED as the Infinite nature of its source.

It was by Inspiration that all truth has been discovered whether in Science, Philosophy, Morals or Religion. It is not meant that in any instance there has been miraculous inspiration, contrary to, or above, the general laws of nature; but simply, that God has so organized the human mind, as to enable it, in the progress of life, to discover new Truth.

It is not material to the subject, to determine, whether the SOURCE of Life acts through laws which constitute the forms of vital manifestation; or whether His Spirit is immediately present in all forms. Whether it is through the medium of laws controlling the organization of matter and mind, or from the immediate, informing presence of the DIVINE MIND, it is equally true that our JUST conceptions flow from God!

It is the province of the human mind to grasp the phenomena of Nature; to explore its history; to take cognizance of its expression; and to turn upon itself, and reflect upon its own laws, analyze its own powers, and to strive to discover the meaning of this wonderful state of being. In all ages and climes, this DIVINE INSTINCT of the human mind, however thwarted (§) has sought the GOOD, the BEAUTIFUL, the TRUE;

---

*The genuine dictates of our natural faculties is the *voice of God*, no less than what He reveals from Heaven.—*Reid's Philosophy.*

§ According to the German Philosophers, God is conceived as the absolute and original Being revealing himself variously in outward nature and in human intelligence and freedom. It is not easy to see how pantheism, in this sense, differs from the Christian view of God, as expressed in the sublime language of St. Paul, "In whom we live and move and have our being." —*Brande.*

to discover its Source—comprehend its nature and to explore its destiny. Here and there, in the long ages, brilliant lights have shot athwart the mental sky, dispersing the clouds of error and illustrating the persistence and energy of the Divine Instinct—an Instinct of exhaustless energy—one that can never cease to prosecute the discovery of Truth---never rest, while anything remains unknown, of Man, of Nature or of God.*

THE ULTIMATE TRUTH IN SCIENCE.

Scientists say that "all the pnenomena of Nature can be traced to the laws of Matter." Science is founded upon accurately observed facts and many such facts are required to establish an indubitable truth, and in view of this, some doubt may rest upon the judgment, as the postulate is broad, covering indeed, the highest generalization of physical science.

It is not said, however, that all phenomena can be traced to MATTER, but, to the LAWS of matter, and, the postulate being thus evidently true, a knowledge of the LAWS of NATURE becomes a subject of the profoundest interest to the human mind.

Let us glance at these laws, at least at the general laws or FORCES of NATURE. Probably with nebulous matter the counteracting tendencies of the law of gravitation gave to the great globes of space their form and their movements, and evidently Heat, Light and Electricity, were agencies in the evolution of vegetable life. But these forces, if not produced by matter could have had no effect without it, and though essential as media, let us see if they are not subordinate to a higher FORCE. Let us contemplate THAT as a LAW or FORCE clearly recognizable to the human mind.

Science has traced the laws of Nature back to the "mysterious ether" pervading space; to the nebulous matter or "fire mist" of the astronomer; to the atoms of

---

* "One great object," says Hallam, "that most of the Schoolmen had in view was to establish the principles of natural theology by abstract reasoning. * But all discovery of truth by means of such a controversy was rendered hopeless by two insurmountable obstacles: (the authority of Aristotle and the Church.) * After three or four hundred years the Scholastics had not untied a single knot, nor added one unequivocal truth to the domain of philosophy. How different is the state of genuine philosophy, the zeal for which will never wear out by length of time or change of fashion, because the inquirer, unrestrained by authority, is perpetually cheered by the discovery of truth in researches which the boundless riches of nature seem to render indefinitely progressive.—*Middle Ages, p's. 527'8*

the chemist, or, the molecules of the physicist. It can go no farther—trace no farther matter or its forces.

And yet, there is another FORCE paramount, and over-ruling all others and the atoms of matter in all their combinations. A FORCE physical science recognizes, as far as science treads, as preceding all observation of the molecules, and forming in its control of other forces, the worlds of space. A Force which entered into inorganic matter and controlled the movements of the molecules in all their combinations—informed the chrystals—and clothed itself in living forms out of the Primitive Rocks. Name it as you will—"instinct of the molecules," "the law of selection," the principle of "attraction and repulsion," "reason," "intellect," "wisdom," all the same, as either expression exhibits the manifestation of the INTELLECTUAL FORCE in Nature, which, through matter, has clothed itself successively in the vegetable, the fish, the reptile, mammalia, and lastly, in man, the highest and most complete concentration of the over-ruling FORCE of Nature.

"The fifty-five elementary substances into which the solid liquids and aeriform fluids of the earth have been reduced, observe, in their combinations, certain mathematical proportions. One volume of them unites with one, two, three, or more volumes, of another, any quantity being sure to be left over if such there should be. It is hence supposed that matter, composed of infinitely minute particles or atoms, each belonging to any one substance, can only, *through the operation of some hidden law*, associate with a certain number of the atoms of any other."

"An influence," says Herschel, "is apparent not only in the matter of the earth, but the worlds of space, giving them all the same direction, a *family likeness*, as they move in order around some great centre of the infinite universe."

"Law," said Humboldt, "is the supreme rule of the universe, and that law is wisdom, is intellect, is reason. whether reviewed in the formation of Planetary systems, or in the organization of the worm."—*Kosmos*.

** "From the consideration of ourselves and what we infallibly find in our own constitutions our reason leads us to the knowledge of this certain and evident truth, that there is an eternal. most powerful and most knowing Being which, whether any one will please to call God, matters not."—*Locke.*

We cannot become too familiar with this FORCE, Go back to the molecules or the "mysterious ether" and you find that it it is a FORCE IN but not OF matter.

We trace matter to the immaterial, the inscrutable, and still find the FORCE an ACTIVE POWER. Follow it from the molecules up to man and you find that it is instinct, thought, intellect, reason, reflection, memory, perpetually IMPELLED in search of better and higher expression. Scientists name it the "law of selection." It would be more definite to call it the selecting Force, or better still, the DIRECTING, INFORMING and ADVANCING FORCE of Nature.

"Atoms and molecules," says the chemist, "arrange themselves under the influence of chemical and chrystalic laws, into geometrical shapes and thus the solid rocks of the earth were formed." Elementary substances unite in definite proportions and form their physical combinations in obedience to the instinct pervading all nature, informing all matter. With matter organized, that instinct becomes the conservator of life. It adapts the organized being to its environment, and supplies, subject to that environment, its wants. In all the orders of nature, vegetable and animal, every atom is moved by the same FORCE, the same instinct, seeking that which is necessary to the organization. Follow it from the vegetable to the quadruped and from the latter to man, and you see it moving the tender roots of the plant in search of food; moving the brute in search of its appropriate aliment and moving man in a like pursuit, the FORCE, in all instances, adapted to the organization, subject to its environment.

It appears, then, that to this FORCE, as it is imparted to matter, may be traced all the phenomena of nature. "As IT IS IMPARTED TO MATTER!" The *Fauna and Flora* of the Polar, Temperate and Torrid Zones differ. Montesquieu tells us truly that the laws, manners, habits and customs of man differ from climatic influences. If such is the effect of the Sun upon development, physical and mental, how natural that the emanations, the rays, the gleams of the mental FORCE of the Universe—the Source of Intellect—should produce diversified expression, especially when we know that inert matter is its medium.

That there is then an INTELLECTUAL FORCE pervading and over-ruling all Nature, is abundantly sustained by all the facts of Science and the observations of common sense.

THE ULTIMATE TRUTH IN PHILOSOPHY.

What is this INTELLECT? It led the writer of the Book of Job to seek its great ORIGINAL in a SUPREME RULER, not unlike the INTELLECT of the writer. It led, as vainly, all subsequent thought, to seek, not a SPIRIT, not a FORCE in Nature—but a GREAT ARCHITECT, who moulded the forms of matter as man moulds his wares, and looking at these forms, defective and conflicting in their environment, and expressive of GOOD AND EVIL, THEOLOGY was brought to the inconsistency that GOD is no-where, and every-where. If we will reflect that HE is no-where, except as an INTELLECTUAL FORCE and that every-where, HE is that FORCE, the problem is solved. If we will reflect that HE is the INFORMING and DIRECTING SPIRIT of the Infinite Universe of matter, of WHOM we can never know more than our minds can comprehend; WHO is never present to us except as thus comprehended, through everywhere, whether conceived or not. That though he is present with the ant, the sparrow, and they know it not; yet you may know that He is present with them and with yourself. Then while we admire the exhibition of this great FORCE, in chemical and animal laws; while we repeat:

"What though in solemn silence all,
Move round this great terrestrial ball;
In reason's ear they all rejoice
And utter forth a glorious voice,
Forever singing as they shine
The hand that made us is Divine."

While thus impressed, we will be most deeply moved by the exhibition of the FORCE in man, in whom we find the highest earthly exposition of DIVINITY—INTELLECT reflecting upon its SOURCE—reflecting upon the MENTAL illumination of the universe.

"That lives through all life, extends thro' all extent,
Spreads undivided, operates unspent."

Aristotle said "there are two elements in Nature, MIND and MATTER." Mind must have come from mind and the Intellect of man, though material its organs of expression, is a FORCE making its way through, and forcing matter, to lend itself to the evolution of something higher—infinitely higher than the dark material it employs—to the evolution of broader intellectual views, of greater love, higher life and better conditions of existence.

The physical organization is resolved into the molecules or atoms of matter, of which it is composed and the instincts that impelled, having served their uses, perish with it when the organization is dissolved. The INTELLECT—the desire for knowledge, the power to think, to reason, to reflect, with its delight in wisdom in goodness and the beautiful, actually hoping for and seeking some higher form of existence, belongs not to the organization, but is immortal and must return to the Source from whence it came.

It is rational to accept the evidence of our senses, and with Des Carte CONSCIOUSNESS, as the foundation of knowledge. We find THAT to be the essential spirit of SELF, a quality of mind shared, according to the requirements of organization, by all the forms of animated nature. The Mimosa shrinks from adverse contact; the animal shuns danger and man, not only conscious of existence and thought, distinctly asserts in the EGO his identity, his individuality, whether wisely or unwisely, depends upon the INTELLECTUAL FORCE received, or, as Solomon and Locke said, in other words "upon the understanding."

MATTER has had its evolution, its progress in the "history of the rocks," but not more distinctly, or certainly, than MIND. With all the advances of organic life, mind has expanded, developed, until, in man, we find in exercise, not only the instincts of the lower animals, but reason, judgment, reflection and the CONSCIOUSNESS of these mental operations.

But these are not all the mental qualities diffused through the mind of man, by the INTELLECTUAL FORCE, as reflection will readily suggest. DESIRE is the impelling principle of the INTELLECTUAL FORCE, and with instinct and intellect to inform, animates all nature. In lower life DESIRE is confined to the wants of the animal organization. In man it is never satisfied with the gratification of these wants but is forever reaching out for something above them—something purer and better. Nor does the INSPIRATION stop here. DESIRE becomes exciting EMOTION and urges the Intellect forward in search of "the way, the truth and the light." It spans, with HOPE the chasm between time and the infinite, and with fitful, but not unmeaning flashes, portrays the pleasing imageries of the state of the blessed.

This MIND, this DESIRE, this HOPE, this IMAGINATION is the OUT-FLOW through Nature of the INTELLECTUAL FORCE.

"All are but parts of one stupendous whole,
Whose body Nature is and GOD the soul."

"Else whence this pleasing hope, this fond desire
this longing after immortality, if 'tis not "the divinity
that stirs within us."

"There is a Divinity that shapes our ends, rough hew them as
we may."

"In whom we live, and move, and have our being."--*Paul.*

"God is a spirit and must be worshiped in spirit and in truth."

The INTELLECTUAL FORCE, in its highest earthly development, carries with it the emotions of the mind,
and if the soul of man is immortal, it is because its capacity and aspirations are higher than mere brutal or
physical wants. The highest possible evidence of that
immortality is the FACT that it is HOPE and Expectation
INSPIRED by the INTEI LECTUAL FORCE.

Whether as Budha or Brahma taught, the INTELLEC-
TUAL FORCE in man will be re-absorbed; or as Sacrates
taught, "we will be hearth-fellows with the Gods," or as
others have taught, "Angels of light," we know not
yet. Science has DEMONSTRATED that the INTELLECTUAL
FORCE in Nature has impelled its own evolution—its development, from the molecules, through all the changes
of matter, to man. But it is asked, "if the brain is the
organ of expression here, how is the INTELLECTUAL FORCE
to express itself hereafter? If you assert that matter is
eternal, (though that is a postulate beyond your conception,) you will not deny the eternity of the INTEL-
LECTUAL FORCE, which moves, animates, informs, and directs it, and you will consider, that this FORCE has found
its expression IN NATURE, and will not deny that it must
find that expression FOREVER. You will also consider
that its mode of expression has exhibited PERSISTENT ex
pansion—enlargement, and will hardly deny, that after
so many ages of growing illumination, it can find no
HIGHER MEDIUM than the matter with which we are ac-
quainted. We possess a consciousness here of thought
and emotion higher than necessary to THIS existence;
but we cannot have the consciousness of ANOTHER, until
we reach it. The worm is conscious of existence. In
the chrysalis consciousness is suspended. In the but-
terfly it is revived; but it is the consciousness of the but-
terfly, not that of the worm.

It is thus we KNOW, from observation, reason and
consciousness that a great INTELLECTUAL POWER—SOURCE

of all thought, all wisdom, all love, and all loveliness, reigns supreme in the universe of matter, and while almost assured of immortal happiness we rest in confident hope, KNOWING ourselves safe

"With one disposing Power,
Or in the natal or the mortal hour."

When, (regarding man from the stand-point of the materialist,) we pass through this nether-most scene of animated nature; when we have tasted life's little round of animal pleasures; when we have borne physical pain until the system groans beneath the burden of life; when the pleasures of sense are dulled, and the pains of sense prevail; when pleasurable emotions are stilled, or succeeded by those of mental suffering following the wreck of life's endearments, when we see and feel this life, as it is, "a fleeting illusion," in which there is nothing permanent- nothing satisfying; when thus enlightened, we turn from it mournfully accepting the verdict of mankind:

I would not live alway, I ask not to stay
Where storm after storm rises dark o'er my way."

"Shadows we are, and shadows we pursue."

"Like bubbles on the sea of matter borne,
And to that sea return."

"Man was made to mourn."

"Those whom the God's love die young."—*Greek proverb.*

'The boast of heraldry, the pomp of power,
All that beauty, all that wealth e'er gave
Await alike, the inevitable hour
The paths of glory lead but to the grave."

"Life's a stage and men and women merely players."

"We are such stuff as dreams are made of."

"How weary, stale flat and unprofitable,
Are all the uses of this life"

To-morrow, and to-morrow, and to-morrow,
Creeps in this petty pace from day to day
To the last syllable of recorded time,
And all our yesterday's have lighted fools
The way to dusty death."

But, when we find in this life something worthy of the highest REASON; when we find developed in our own being, a SPIRIT, animated with the DESIRE and INSTINCT of immortality, which even now turns with loathing from the gross pleasures of sense, and, fixed in the conception of a nature infinite, looks forward to the SPIRIT LIFE, as its natural home—as its proper stage of being—as duly succeeding in the order of Nature, an inferior condition of PROGRESSIVE LIFE; when we are thus aroused to our highest earthly capacity, we find the solution of life's problem—the balm for all our woes—the fruition of all our hopes, and the inspiration of God's infinite WISDOM and LOVE.

"Throw aside then all silliness of this kind, and think upon this, that after the union of soul with body has been once dissolved by the former being settled in its own home place, what is left of the latter is of the earth and devoid of reason, nor is it a man. For we are a soul; a thing of life and immortal, pent up in a mortal prison."—SOCRATES.

"When we are at home with the body we are absent from the Lord, but when we are absent from the body we are present with the Lord."—PAUL.

With Science and Philosophy in perfect harmony—mutually grounded upon the immutable FACTS of Nature, we read with heightened pleasure the INTUITION of the poet:

"Let every living soul,
Beneath the spacious temple of the sky,
In adoration join; and ardent raise,
One general song! To him ye vocal gales,
Breathe soft, whose spirit in your freshness breathes;
Oh, talk of Him in solitary glooms;
Where o'er the rock, the scarcely waving pine
Fills the brown shade with a religious awe.
And ye whose bolder note is heard afar
Who shake the astonished world, lift high to Heaven
Th' impetuous song and say from whom you rage.
His praise, ye brooks attune, ye trembling rills,
And let me catch it as I muse along.
Ye headlong torrents, rapid and profound;
Ye softer floods, that lead the humid maze;
Along the vale; and thou majestic main,
A secret world of wonders in thyself,
Sound his stupendous praise, whose greater voice
Or bids you roar or bids your roarings fall.
Soft roll your incense. herbs and fruits, and flowers,
In mingled clouds to Him whose Sun exhalts.
Whose breath perfumes you, and whose pencil paints.
Ye forests bend, ye harvests wave to Him;
Breathe your still song into the reaper's heart
As home he goes beneath the joyous moon.
Ye that keep watch in Heaven, as earth asleep
Unconscious lies, effuse your mildest beams,
Ye constellations, while your angels strike
Amid the spangled sky, the silver lyre.
Great source of day! best image here below
Of thy Creator; ever pouring wide
From world to world, the vital ocean round;

On nature write with every beam his praise,
The thunder rolls: be hush'd the prostrate world
While cloud to cloud returns the solemn hymn,
Bleat out afresh ye hills: ye mossy rocks,
Retain the sound: the broad responsive low
Ye valleys raise; *for the Great Shepherd Reigns;*
And his unsuffering Kingdom *yet will come.*
Ye woodlands all awake: a boundless song
Burst from the groves: and when the restless day,
Expiring, lays the warbling world asleep,
Sweetest of birds, sweet Philomela charm
The listening shades and teach the night his praise.
Ye Chief, for whom the whole Creation smiles,
At once the head and heart, and tongue of all,
Crown the great hymn: in swarming cities vast,
Assembled men, to the deep organ join
The long resounding voice, oft breaking clear
At solemn pauses, through the swelling base
And, as each mingling flame increases each,
In one united ardor rise to Heaven.
Or, if you rather choose the rural shade,
And find a fane in every secret grove,
There let the Shepherd's flute, the Virgin's lay,
The prompting seraph, and the poet's lyre
Still sing the God of seasons, as they roll.
For me, when I forget the darling theme
Whether the blossom blows, the summer ray
Russets the plain, inspiring autumn gleams,
Or winter rises in the blackening east;
Be my tongue mute, my fancy paint no more,
And dead to joy, forget my heart to beat.
Should fate command me to the farthest verge
Of the green earth to distant barbarous climes,
Rivers unknown to song; where first the Sun
Gilds Indian Mountains, or his setting beam,
Flames on the Atlantic isles; 'tis naught to me
Since God is ever present, ever felt,
In the void waste as in the city full,
And where he vital breathes, there must be joy.
When even at last the solemn hour shall come
And wing my mystic flight to future worlds,
I cheerful will obey; then with new powers,
Will rising wonders sing. I cannot go
Where universal love not smiles around
Sustaining all yon orbs, and all their suns
From seeming ill still enducing good
And better thence again and better still
In infinite progression.

THE RELIGIOUS INSTINCT.

Religion is faith (or belief) in a Supreme Power, and an inspiration of the Intellectual Force, and, therefore, a mental expression of the mind of man. In the various degrees of intellectual development, as illustrated in modes of religion,

there is a principle of harmony common to all—an eternal
foundation upon which they all rest—the impulse of the Intellectual Force, which has persistently pointed man to

> "The FATHER of all in every age,
>   In every clime adored,
> By saint, by savage, and by sage—
>   Jehovah, Jove or Lord."

The conception of the Great Spirit has varied in all ages
as expressed through the mind of man, and yet in all ages
and climes the expression declares complete identity in the
great Truth underlying each conception. No one conception
can be said to be derived from another save the derivation of
the conception of Moses from the Egyptians and that of Ma-
homet from Moses. All other conceptions of the Great Spirit
were *inspirations*. Obliterate all conception of God from
the mind of man and the inspiration will again come, again
find voice, varied as before, by organism and environment.

Before the Pyramids were built the Egyptians represented
the Supreme Being as carrying on a constant conflict with
the Spirit of Evil.

Zoroaster said, "There is one God, and not many gods."
"There are two forces in nature, opposed to each other, good
and evil."

> "What God shall we adore with sacrifice?
> Him let us praise, the golden child that rose
> In the beginning, who was born the Lord—
> The one sole Lord of all that is—who made
> The earth and formed the sky, who giveth life,
> Who giveth strength, whose bidding gods revere,
> Whose hiding-place is immortality, whose shadow
> Death, who by His might is King of all
> The breathing, sleeping, waking world—
> *Who is the breath of life of all that lives.*"
>   —*Bible of the Hindus.*

> "Far in the deep infinitudes of space
> Upon a throne of silence, when chaos reigned,
> Was the Lord of the center of the universe."
>   —*Japanese Religion.*

The Chinese sacrifice to Shan-te, the Supreme Ruler, or
God. To this Supreme Being all the highest forms of adoration have been offered for 2,300 years B. C. In His hands
were the issues of life and death, and he whom He blessed
was blessed, and he whom He cursed was cursed. The Tao-
ists of the Chinese hold to a *materialistic* religion—that the
soul is evolved from matter, gaining immortality by trans-
mutation. The Budhists are *metaphysical*, denying the existence of matter, and holding that the world of the senses is
ideal.

"I believe Thee to be best Being of all, the source of light for all
the world. Every one shall choose Thee as the source of light.

Thee, O Mazda, most beneficent spirit. Thou created'st all good, true things by means of the power of Thy good mind."
—*Parsee Bible.*

The Druids of England, tracing their religion back to the days of Noah, had several words expressive of their conception of the Supreme Being: " God," " Distributor," " Governor," " The Mysterious One," " The Eternal," "He that pervadeth all things," " The Author of existence." They taught that " God cannot be matter ; what is not matter is God."

It will be observed that while all religions recognize, in the perpetual conflict of good and evil, the prevalence of the Great Spirit, yet, that none of them represent the human soul as the highest earthly expression of that spirit, or as an emanation from it. That was reserved for higher inspiration fully expressed in the beginning and closing words of the wise and tender prayer—

" Our FATHER, who art in heaven; hallowed be Thy name. Thy kingdom come, Thy will be done, on earth as 'tis done in heaven. * * * For *Thine* is the kingdom, the power and the glory, forever."

We have (as we could) followed the development and growth of the Intellectual Force, through inorganic and organic nature, from the molecules to man, and find in him a capacity of mind awakened to reflect *whence it came.* The conception, as the medium of transmission, has varied, but the Force will continue to develop and enlarge its expression forever.

It was right that the mythologists worshipped the elements ; they reflect the Intellectual Force. It was right that Zoroaster worshipped the sun; it reflects the Intellectual Force. It is right that the Positivists worship high mental development, as great men exhibit in the highest degree, the Intellectual Force. Budha, musing in solitude, had the Force of Mental Illumination in bright effulgence cast upon him ; and it is above all things right that man should discover more fully the true object of worship through Jesus Christ, as in the highest degree was evolved in him the Intellectual Force, which, in its last analysis, is Wisdom and Love.

In transmitting light, we look to the medium. As with other forces, the intellectual has its resisting medium. Inertia of the molecules—the appetites, passions and propensities of animal nature, suppress, distort or pervert the transmission of the intellectual light. But the result is manifestly, orderly progress. which it has gradually extended through all the changes and convulsions of matter until the primitive rocks were formed, when matter, earth, sea and air, were all combined, with the laws of nature, in the production of organized life, when the Force exhibited itself as instinct, which, gradually expanding through all the orders of animated nature, finally unfolded its true essence in man, in whom it has since persistently widened and extended its diffusion until we are justified by reason in the hope that man will advance on earth to a much higher expression of Wisdom and Love.

Rising above all animal depravity is the Intellectual Force. Though necessary in degree to vegetable and animal forms, these were not its ends, nor did the growth stop, with the coming of man, in the poor purpose of nourishing the body through a brief and objectless existence. It forced him to cultivate Art and to investigate Nature, to learn that Wisdom, Intellect, Reason, prevails, and that he might be lifted up to a full sense of humanity, love for man in whom the light shines or may shine, and love for the Force that imparts it.

Reflect upon the mental capacity of man ; upon that " wondrous thinking thing, the human mind ;" a mental *ego*, that thinks, judges, reasons, excited by emotions of infini e anticipations ; of the mental power of reflection—a faculty of the mind that reviews its own operations, and, as we are doing now, its own history, and sees—

> " Far as the heavens had birth
> The spirit trace its rising track "—

Until it has grown, expanded, developed, evolved, in that greatest of all phenomena, the human mind.

When Newton observed the apple fall, it was not until after laborious thought, profound reflection, that he was led to the discovery of a great law of nature. But even that great and early force, operating in matter, is controlled by another equally as well defined, equally pervading in matter—"attraction and repulsion." There was, before the law of gravitation, a force that gave to the unseen ether filling all space, to the fire-mist, to the atoms and molecules, " attraction and repulsion." In other words there was, in the beginning, the Intellectual Force.

Now accept the law of development, of evolution. You will not think of rejecting its grandest feature, its most wonderful efflorescence, the fruit by which, alone, all the works of nature were made *conceivable*. You will consider, indeed, above all phenomena, the evolution of mind, of intellect. Begin, if you choose, with the laws of attraction and repulsion, formative instincts of the molecules, and follow these laws through all their instinctive exhibitions in vegetable and animal life until you find them so wonderfully unfolded in man. You then find that these instincts have developed faculties suited to the advanced organization. You witness the development of judgment, reason, reflection, in obedience still to the impulsive instinct. You follow man through all stages of his development, from savage to pastoral, pastoral to agricultural and commercial, from ignorance to science, art and civilization, and development (evolution) becomes the evident law of mental as of phyiscal progress.

Accept the facts of physical science, but let us observe the highest natural law, the highest force of nature, the impelling and informing Force of Intellect, as it is to this we are indebted for all that is conceived in matter, all that is estimable in knowledge, all that is elevating in morals, all that is aspiring in mind.

The Intellectual Force is just as natural as the law of gravitation, and, like the light of the sun, diffuses itself through all matter. The reception of the Force depends upon the organism and its environment. All the forces of nature operate through resisting mediums, and all that we call evil in life (physical and moral) results from this fact. Just as you see the flora of nature every-where struggling with its environment for existence; as you see its fauna every-where struggling to maintain life; as you see man, through all the centuries, struggling to better his condition; just so you see the Intellectual Force within him, how it has impelled, developed and expanded until it has reached, through a dark medium, its present evolution.

Distinguish the two natures—Matter and Mind—and, first, reflect that organized matter subsists *by feeding upon itself.*

" All forms that perish other forms supply,
By turns we catch the vital breath and die."

The rocks decay and accumulate the elements upon which vegetation subsists, and that, in turn, becomes the food of animal life, which, in its turn, largely subsists upon itself. It is conjectured that man in the early stages of his history was as certainly under the dominion of animal instinct as the brute, and he is yet gramnivorous, carnivorous, omnivorous, with all the organic desires distinguishing lower life.

This is blind matter, with just enough of the Intellectual Force to preserve animal organization. The food of the mind (of the soul), on the other hand, is knowledge, truth; the soul growing by what it feeds on, and every point gained exciting more strongly the love of the *beautiful*, the *true*, and the *good*, finding its satisfaction only in a table spread vast as eternity.

"Whosoever drinketh of the water that I shall give him shall never thirst, but the water that I shall give him shall be in him a well of water springing up into eternal life."

The poet says the angels exhibited Newton to curious audiences " as we show an ape." Newton compared himself to a little child gathering pebbles on the beach of an infinite ocean.

Know thyself! and say if there is nothing within you but the animal. Mr. Spencer is exhibiting the close resemblance of the anatomy of man and the dog. He can go farther, and trace that resemblance from man to the lowest form of the vertebrata. And observation would lead him, still farther, to find it exhibited in the *features* of man ; and farther still, to find man animated by every instinct, in varied degree, as if the progenitors of all, with Romulus and Remus, had been suckled by a wolf—voracious, fierce, cruel, secretive, deceptive, over-reaching, hypocritical, every animal instinct exaggerated and sometimes refined by superior sagacity, culminating in those twin-monsters of brutality, the love of *power* and the love of *gold*.

> " Ay, in the catalogue ye go for men,
> As hounds and greyhounds, mongrels, spaniels, curs,
> Shoughs, water-rugs, and demi wolves are 'cleped
> All by the name of dogs; the valued file
> Distinguishes the swift, the slow the subtle,
> The housekeeper the hunter—every one
> According to the gift which bounteous nature
> Hath in him closed."

Is this all of man? Have you no consciousness of anything higher and better in your nature? True, when one is successful in reaching the highest ambition of the animal instincts his *ego*, his " I myself," becomes dreadfully distended ; but it does (and ought to) meet the fate of the fabled Frog.

Popular clamor, in each generation, in every nation, city and hamlet, makes its ephemeral great men. Briefly, the great men and the fools pass away together and are forgotten. But when the Intellectual Force fully develops a great man—when Socrates braves death for truth, or Jesus the crucifixion, or Bruno the stake, or Gallileo persecution—a great *mind* is produced whose light is never extinguished.

The history of mind, in man, is the persistent effort of the Intellectual Force to subdue animal instinct and to subordinate the laws of matter, organic and inorganic, to *rational* uses. This has been the burthen of philosophy and religion as it is of science. This was the great intellectual conflict of the Greeks ; this the animation of the Roman moralists ; this that brought to human conception the mariner's compass, the printing press, the power to subdue to human uses the solar rays and the forked lightning ; and this it was

2

that, in the midst of Egyptian darkness, surrounded by the profound mental depravity of his people, that inspired Moses with the conception of higher *intelligence*, of a higher *power* than matter, of a *wisdom* greater than man's mere brutal instincts. It was the conception of Moses, and it detracts not from its *truth* that the Power, as conceived, was not unlike Moses himself.

"Stick not in the bark." That was the error of Paine, the French school, Gibbon and others. Rejecting the garb, they discarded the spirit. Tearing down a shelter and turning the family out of doors, exposed to the peltings of the pitiless storm, before erecting a new one. They did not reflect that the Intellectual Force had evolved through organized matter until it reached its development in man, where it is still encompassed with its resisting medium, physical nature and its instincts. They did not reflect that it came to us, not only through this dark medium, but to communicate itself to the general mind, in all ages, it passed through many and changeable languages, through many transcriptions, finding the latter medium as dark and distorting as the first.

FORMULATED RELIGION.

In all the ages of man the spirit of Religion has assumed form, the modes of worship varying with the conception of the Intellectual Force. In all of them the *object* worshiped has grown in illumination, and yet all are defective, all too much animated by the animal instincts. Still, they are conservative of truth, of the spirit of Nature, of the voice of God, though, while holding fast to the progress of the past, they always become a bar, an obstacle, to the advancement of the Intellectual Force, but to which they all find they must, sooner or later, subordinate themselves or perish.

"Truth crushed to earth will rise again,
The eternal years of God are hers;
But error, wounded, writhes in pain,
And dies amid its worshipers."

Corrupt generally, cruel often, has formulated religion been in its domination of man. It sentenced Socrates to death for uttering *truth ;* it crucified Jesus Christ; it burnt Bruno at the stake, and many other martyrs, and has been the moving cause of most of the wars and social desolations of modern times. But the truths of Socrates and Bruno continue to enlighten the mind of man, and the words of Jesus *live.* " Whited sepulchre, full of corruption and dead men's bones." Form may bar itself against the Intellectual Force diffused and diffusing through nature; but even its own passions, mingled with higher aims, serve the evolution of the Intellectual Force, as when Gallileo broke a pane of glass and let the light pour in, and Luther unlocked the door and let the light pour out.

When the light forced its way out for general diffusion, zealots encompassed "in dead men's bones" lit their rush-lights from the flame, and each, waving them aloft, exclaimed, "Behold the true light!" and, instead of one form of relig-ion we have a dozen, involved, at first, in fierce and bloody strife; throughout, in bitter contention; all, in obedience to animal instinct—the love of power and the love of gold.

Abolish not the *form*, but drive out or subordinate the brute. As Jesus attempted to cleanse the Jewish temple, go into Turkish mosque, Christian church or Indian temple and cleanse them of all brutality, of all animal propensity, and subordinate them to advancing intelligence and the pure meditations of the soul. Fancy not that He can be cribbed, confined, by work of human hands, but *know* that He is with you at all times and places, as your minds are framed for the reception of His spirit, which fills, directs, informs, the boundless universe of nature. This is His temple, the solar and the astral worlds, farther than eye can see or glass can reach, and this, in every accessible department and in all its relations, is the proper study of mankind, as it is the only possible medium of inspiration. It is well to worship the Great Source of Intellect; to seek His wisdom and love, one day in the week; but far better, while living a life of useful-ness, as far as in you lies, to live daily in the consciousness of His informing presence. Banish the miraculous and su-pernatural with all authority devoid of useful and evident truth, relying no more upon "dead men's bones" than to extract from them evidence of the gradual diffusion and de-velopment in nature of the Spirit of God. Let Philosophy teach by historical example, from the origin of man to his present moral and intellectual estate, from his beginning in barbarism to his present outgrowth of civilization, the devel-opment and diffusion of that Spirit. Trace Language, from signs and gestures, to its present capacity of conveying, from mind to mind, conceptions of the beautiful and sublime. The Arts, from their origin in caves and tents and rude im-plements, to all the comforts, elegancies, utilities, conven-iences and delights they now afford. Let Science teach the diffusion of the Intellectual Force through matter, inorganic and then organic, until the table was spread for man, and then follow man through his conflicts with adverse nature, through habits, manners, customs, government and religion, to find the *spirit* exhibited in its present earthly Force, and we will readily conceive its wonderful excellence, its progressive diffusion and inevitable tendency. Let the scientist, the truth-seeking "skeptic," the follower of Budha, Brahma, Moses and Jesus Christ all meet together in joyful communion, every animal instinct and propensity subdued, "to drink of the water freely given" and be "born again;" to send up united invocation for increase of the Intellectual Force; for the Divine Afflatus; for the inspiration of the Comforter and the Holy Ghost; for the coming more and more of His kingdom, the dominion of Wisdom and Love, and then "through the long-drawn aisle and fretted vault, the pealing anthem," in symphony with the intellect and emotions of the soul, will swell, indeed, "the note of praise;" for Music, "heavenly maid," is the Spirit of Harmony, mourning the adversities of life and exulting in its joys.

Let the Church reform its auxiliary schools. "Train up the child in the way it should go," but bandage not its intellect with effete dogmas, as "the way it should go" is not according to arbitrary formulas constructed with a view to ecclesiastical power; but to the free and untramelled exercise of intellectual energy. The grandest thoughts of man have not found expression, yet, in language. The brightest effulgence of the Intellectual Force has not, yet, found expression through matter. Hence we are taught to pray, "Thy kingdom come, Thy will be done on earth as it is in heaven." Teach the child this *end* of human mental *desire*, and instruct him that the laws of nature, properly understood, lead to it, and the intellectual progress of the race will be wonderfully accelerated.*

As the light came to Budha, and to Socrates, so it came to Moses. Contemplating the miseries of mankind under the dominion of animal instinct, depravity became apparent as the status of the race. Reflection taught him that man was capable of higher aims and a nobler life under the dominion of Intelligence, Reason, Wisdom, and from these qualities as they operated in his own mind he, inferred an Intellectual Source as their origin. It matters not how he sought to impress this Intelligence, Reason, Wisdom, upon an ignorant people, buried mentally beneath the weight of the animal instincts. We are only concerned with the fact of his inspiration—the conception of the natural depravity of man—

---

* See "Combe on the Constitution of Man."

his higher capabilities, and an overruling Intellectual Power in Nature. Everything else ascribed to him may be discarded, except one other inspiration, great as all these—an inspiration which has come in no other way in nature to man—which founded, at once and forever, upon the highest possible human conception of the Intellect, Wisdom and Love that overrules the universe, the moral law of man.

The search is vain, in the absence of a higher intellectual power in nature than man, to find a foundation for moral law. All effort in this direction has ended "in the consent of the governed"—"conventionalism—"there is nothing either right or wrong, but thinking makes it so." Science has done as yet no better—found nothing higher than expediency to which to refer the great issues of right and wrong, and under its now familiar phrase, "the survival of the fittest," right and wrong, in nature become matters of indifference where expediency and success, whether of individuals or races, are the highest sanctions of law.

Moral law for man, it is true, cannot transcend his intelligence; but, in the highest human intelligence, it finds for him its foundation, and, the knowledge that that intelligence is progressive in development, and, that it could come from no other than an infinitely intelligent source, moral law—the distinction of good and evil, of right and wrong, whatever you or I may think, finds its foundation in the overruling force of nature.

Crude, coarse, erroneous, much that is ascribed to Moses appears to the skeptic ; but the great facts with which he was inspired will not be denied ; the depravity of man ; his capacity for progressive mental development ; the recognition of intellect, reason, wisdom, in himself, in nature, and in the source from whence they must have proceeded ; and in his final conception of moral law, based upon the relation of the human intellect to that source.

It was a very simple, natural and rational operation of the human mind that gave inspiration to Budha, Zoroaster and to Moses. A well developed mind cannot avoid observing among mankind, and reflecting upon, exhibitions of pleasure and pain ; enjoyment and delight ; sickness, sorrow, suffering and death ; in a word upon good and evil, and a rational being cannot avoid referring these to a cause, and the varied conception of that cause has furnished the foundation of all the religions of the earth. Moses and others, conceived the cause of evil to be a malignant spirit, perpetually involving the economy of nature in conflict with the cause of the good.

However defective the conception, Budha and Moses found what they sought, a basis for moral law, without which the mind of man is lost in the wilderness of brutality.

The conception of this law is the highest excellence of the human intellect as it is the expressed desire of the Intellectual Force, impelling man to higher knowledge of the true relations of intellect with intellect, and the objects of the law are wisdom, and then, righteousness, and then, beneficence, and aiding to these, are patience, hope and charity, all ending in a mind disenthralled of animal dominion, in a spirit purified.

Let us then base at once and forever, moral obligation, upon the paramount and eternal force 'of nature. What constitutes the "fitest," who survive? Looking at the animal races what does the intellectual force determine as the fitest? At first, strongly armed with weapons of destruction, the roar of the Carnivora filled the gentler animals upon which they fed with terror. Which has survived? Vast flocks and herds of useful and inoffensive animals, feed upon the hills and valleys now, unawed by their terrible enemies. The eagle, fierce, strong and swift, scarce ventures from his inaccessible eyrie to scare the flocks feeding upon the grain of the fields. Follow the development of the law of selec ion until "the table was spread for man." Which of all his races do you find the "fitest?" Do you find them where the animal mostly predominates or the intellectual? Do you not find in the history—the growth of human civilization—that the "fitest" have been those in whom is most fully developed the Intellectual Force, and among these do you not see that this force has evolved the sense of right and wrong, of law, order and benevolence? Then, these are elements of the Intellectual Force. You may see them in the beams of the sun, in the murmuring streams, in the flora that decks the earth, in the songs of the birds, in the affection and providence of animals, in the glee of the harvest, and best of all, in the sentiment of humanity—spreading with the diffusion of the force—alleviating suffering—and in the progress of science and art, lessening the evils and advancing the good of life.

The advancing development of the Intellectual Force is gradual but sure, and it carries along with it, *now,* the sense of right and wrong, of love for all partaking of the force, of humanity, benevolence and moral purity.

" Daily perform thine own appointed work
Unweariedly; and to obtain a friend—
A sure companion to the future world—
Co'lect a store of virtue like the ants.
Who gather up their treasures into heaps;
For neither father, mother, wife nor son,
Nor kinsman will remain beside thee then;
When thou art passing to that other home,
Thy virtue will thy only comrade be.

Single is every living creature born,
Single he passes to another world;
Single he eats the fruit of evil deeds,
Single the fruit of good; and when he leaves
His body, like a log, or heap of clay
Upon the ground, his kins-i en walk away.
Virtue alone stays by him at the tomb,
And bears him through the dreary, trackless gloom."
—*Moral Precepts of the Hindoos.*

THE ULTIMATE TRUTH IN RELIGION,

A THING " OF BEAUTY AND A JOY FOREVER."

The Intellectual Force brought the Egyptian from caves and tents and barbarism, and gave him Architecture, Agriculture, and many useful arts. It took the Hebrew from servile bondage, and, giving to Moses a vague recognition of itself, it gave them their religion, moral and civil law. It impelled the Greek and Roman to preserve all that had been gained and to diffuse and extend, willing or unwilling, the "light of life." Gathering up, through the rise and fall of empires, the intellectual rays, it poured them all into the mind of modern ages, evolving art, science, philosophy, religion, moral and civil law.* Do you not recognize the Overruling Intellectual Force of Nature? Surely, man was *impelled* in all this. Surely, in all this there was a Power moving him, grea er than *his* will, greater than all the empires of man ; a Power subordinating the animal instincts of the race to the gradual development and diffusion of reason, of knowledge, of humanity and religion.

The Intellectual Force lives to-day, in great full ess, in the hearts of many, and should in its brightest earthly purity animate the minds of all mankind, as it is pre-eminent in wisdom, infinite in capacity, perfect in purity, ennobling in its desires, blissful in its hopes, tender in its judgment, merciful and loving in its humanity—emotions that could proceed only from an Intellectual Source of Infinite Perfection.

· As the Force is imparted by its Source in varied degree to

---

* See " History of Civilization."

all nature, so, in more or less fullness, it is imparted in all ages and climes to man. It came to Moses, but with far more brilliant illumination to Jesus Christ. It was his mission to exhibit, as far as the human mind can yet realize, the *dominion* of the animal instincts in man, his capacity for higher mental development, and a just conception of the nature of the Intellectual Force of which the soul of man is an emanation.

Full charged with great and glorious truths, Jesus was met, at the outset, by *formulated prejudice*, asking, "Can anything good come out of Nazareth?" and then by ignorance, immersed in the vices, passions and propensities of brutality through which he sought to impart the love of the Beautiful, the True. the Good; but loving darkness better than light, they crucified him.

John tells us, "In the beginning was Wisdom, (Gibbon's rendering,) and Wisdom was with God, and Wisdom was God. In it was life, and the life was the light of men. It was in the world, and the world was made by it, and the world knew it not. It came unto its own and its own received it not; but as many as received it, to them it gave power to become the *sons of God.*"

Now let science re-write these great truths without change of the sublime thoughts the words convey.

In the beginning was the Intellectual Force, and the Intellectual Force was with God, and the Intellectual Force *was* God. It was life, and the life was the light of men. It was in the world, and the world was made by it, and the world knew it not. It came unto its own and its own received it not; but as many as received it, to them it gave power to become the sons of God.

Now let Philosophy add its attestation: "The soul of man is an emanation of the Divine Mind," and we have Science, Philosophy and Religion, consenting and exulting in the knowledge of the most sublime truth conceivable to man.

The credentials of Jesus Christ, as a bearer of Wisdom, of Intellectual Light, to man, need no appeal to the miraculous or the supernatural for support. What, then, was the new light—the higher Wisdom—so saving, so ennobling, so bright, and yet so imperceptible to others, of which he was the bearer?

His mission was to "bring glad tidings of great joy, with peace on earth and good will among men;" to exhibit to man his true nature; to teach him to know *himself*—that the animal instincts given for physical uses (and mortal as the body) are qualities solely of inferior and transitory nature. This was the *deplored darkness* he came to bring to the recognition of man's Intellect. For this he denounced the hyprocrisy of the Priesthood, the subordination of the Temple to *animal uses*, contrasted the Levite and Samaritan, Dives and Lazarus, and for this that he said "it is easier for a camel to pass through the eye of a needle than for a rich man to enter the kingdom of heaven."

And yet he brought, more fully, the light, that man is capable of something vastly higher and better than this; that he possesses capacity for the reception of a mental Power, if he chooses to receive it, to subordinate all animal instincts to *rational* uses; to subordinate all animal *desire* to the development of Intellectual *desire;* the passing depravity of the brute to knowledge, love and immortality.

He came to teach that this capacity (this Mental Power) is an *inheritance* to all who will receive it, from the Pervading Wisdom, the Divine Spirit of the universe, and is an emanation of that Spirit—the *light* of the Intellectual Force. This light he imparted to all who would receive it, and mourned that so many were debarred by animal depravity from being " gathered together " under its illumination.

He came to exhibit the almost universal depravity of man under the dominion of animal instinct, and denounced, not the instincts themselves; they are natural and necessary to physical health and happiness. It was their *domination* of man, in whatever feature, that he denounced, while he taught that each possessed capacity, in one degree or other, for the dominant Spirit of God—Intellectual *desire* for the love of the Beautiful, the True and the Good—and that when this desire—this love, subordinates animal instinct and dominates the mind, "the man is born again" and becomes with himself " a Son of God."

Bunyan painted the picture with the pencil of faith. Pilgrim, after his passage through trial, suffering and self-denial, appears before the cross, the burden of his animal nature falling from him, and in his happy deliverance starting on his way rejoicing :

"Let cares 'ike a wild deluge come,
 And storms of sorrow fall;
So I but safely reach my home,
 My God, my Heaven, my all."

Upon this desire—this love of the Beautiful, the True and the Good—this expressed Will of God—of the Intellectual Force of Nature, he perfected the moral law of man. "Love thy God with all thy soul and all thy strength, and thy neighbor as thyself." Thus it was proclaimed that the human soul is of essence and nature identical with the wisdom from whence it comes. That it is not only a thinking, knowing, reasoning and emotional essence, but that to perfect itself, to be true to itself, it must grow in moral purity, in love for its Source and love for all partaking of that Source.

It was for the increase of this desire, this love of the Beautiful, the True and the Good, that Jesus prayed,— "Thy *kingdom* come, thy *will* be done, on earth as 'tis done in Heaven." It was this Desire, this Will, this Intellectual Force, to which he patiently submitted his mortal nature. "Nevertheless *Thy will*, not *mine* be done;" and it was this Desire, this Will, this Force, this moving animating Spirit of God, this Supreme Wisdom, embracing, unrestricted, all of its own, that made forgiveness of injuries unlimited, and said "love one another." "Suffer little children to come unto me, and forbid them not for of such is the kingdom of Heaven." "Blessed are the pure in heart for they shall *see* God,"—and finally, to the thief upon the cross, "this night thy soul will be with me in Paradise."

Have we not reached then "the age of Reason, and, founded upon the immutable truths of nature, may not the thousands of millions of passing generations of men, "shout Hozanna to God in the highest?" May they not sing with soul-stirring melody—

> "Peace breathes the comforter, in God's name saying,
> Earth hath no sorrow, Heaven cannot heal."

> "There is a land that is fairer than day,
> And now we can see it afar;
> For the Father waits over the way,
> To prepare us a dwelling place there."

GOOD AND EVIL.

The finite cannot comprehend the infinite, and the eternity of nature is beyond our power of conception; but, far as science can trace the divisibility of matter, *there* is to us the beginning of *facts*.

In the beginning, then, were the molecules, or atoms of matter and inertia. These would have remained forever at rest, without some power, some influence, impelling them to action. That power, that influence, can only be found revealed in the energy of intellect acting upon the inertia of matter.

As the sun diffuses heat through matter, the Impelling Power gave to the atoms the principle of selection—the first manifestation in nature of the Intellectual Force. So that in the beginning there was imparted to matter an over-ruling, directing, controlling Influence, which displayed its power in the formation of the globes of space, the waters, the air, the earth and all organic life; directing the exact proportion of gases to form bodies; directing the roots of plan s in search of food to complete their organization and the animal in a like pursuit, to perfect its organization. As organized life advanced the Influence gradually expanded and developed into desire, and desire into sensation, and sensation into thought, and these, according to organization and environment, are the outflows of the Intellectual Force, impelling and directing all things. To man it gives the ever-impelling principle of life, the desire to better his condition:

"O happiness! our being's end and aim!
Good, pleasure, ease, content, whate'er thy name;
That something still, which prompts the eternal sigh;
For which we bear to live or dare to die."

If you would understand the works of nature, bear in mind that *force* implies *resistance*, and then that the Impelling and Informing Force find its resistance in the inertia of matter. Then you may conceive that the Intellectual Force is, to us, a thing of growth, a thing of purpose, persistently advancing and extending, through the vast period of the earth's duration, from combination to organization; through death to life; compelling the expression, through inert matter, of Wisdom, of Benevolence, of Joy, with the exulting Hope of bringing all things in subjection to itself. You will then, also, readily conceive that resistance to this Force, this Power and its purpose embraces all that we regard as evil in nature.

It is evident then that the Intellectual Force, first recognized by the mind of man in the principle of selection, is the moving, animating, informing, overruling Force of Nature. Toward the "Mysterious Origin" we can only so far safely and securely tread. The beginning, however, of the earth, science has largely brought within the conception of the human mind. Whether formed from nebulous matter or projected from the sun (by the electrical or attractive forces), its beginning was a state of fusion—of liquid fire. When time, of indefinite duration, had cooled its surface, the primitive rocks were formed, and upon them appeared the first forms of *life* and the first exhibition of *instinct.* Let us take the revelations of the Stone Book, and follow their development:

" A partially consolidated planet, tempested by frequent earthquakes of such terrible potency, that those of the historic ages would be but mere ripples of the earth's surface in comparison, could be no proper home for a creature so constituted as man. The fish or reptile—animals of a limited range of instinct, exceedingly tenacious of life in most of their varieties, oviparous, prolific, and whose young, immediately on their escape from the egg, can provide for themselve , might enjoy existence in such circumst nces, to the full extent of their narrow capacities; and when death fell upon them—though their remains, scattered over wide areas, continue to exhibit that distortion of posture incident to violent dissolution, which seems to speak of terror and suffering—we may safe'y conclude that there was but little real suffering in the case. They ere happy up to a certain point, and unconscious forever after. Fishes and reptiles were the proper inhabitants of our planet during the ages o the earth-tempests; and when, under the operation of the chemical laws, these had become less frequent and terrible, the higher mammals were introduced. That prolonged ages of these tempests id exist, and that they gradually settled down, until the state of things became at length comparatively fixed and stable, few geologists will be disposed to deny. The evidence which supports *this* special theory of the development of our planet in its capabilities as a scene of organized and sentient being, seems palpable at every step. Look first at these Grauwacke rocks; and, after marking how in one place the strata have been upturned on their edges for miles together, and how in another the Plutonic rock has risen molten from below, pass on to the Old Red Sandstone, and examine its significant platforms of violent death—its faults, displacements, and dislocations; see, next, in the Coal Measures, those evidences of sinking and ever-sinking strata, for th usands of feet togeth r; mark in the Oolite those vast overlying masses of trap, stretching athwart the landscape, far as the eye can reach; observe c refully how the signs of convulsion and catastrophe *gradually lessen* as we descend to the times of the Tertiary, though even in these ages of the mammiferous quadruped, the earth must have had its oft-recurring ague fits of frightful intensity; and then, on closing the survey, consider how exceedingly *partial* and *unfrequent* these earth-tempests have become in the recent periods. Yes, we find every-where marks of at once *progression* and identity."—*Hugh Miller.*

Identity, in the principles of formation; as the structure of the nerve medium, in all the leading races of animals, is upon the same model; and progress, in the development of this medium, from the lowest form of the vertebrate animals up to man. Progress also in the adaptations of external nature to organized beings. During the Primitive period, the waters, the solid earth and the air were formed, and for ages the latter was so charged with carbonic acid gas that no land animal could breathe it and live. Fish, reptiles and a luxuriant vegetation are the only evidences of life in this vast period of time.

But vegetation fed upon carbon, absorbed it, and in the subsequent convulsions of the earth deposited it where we now find the vast coal-fields, so useful to man. In this vast period of the earth's convulsive changes, from the gases to the rocks, water, air, soil, vegetation and the first forms of animal life, there was no evil, as the medium of sensation had just began its formation. There was disorder and progressive material order, but little sense of pleasure or pain and no *mind* to be elated with thoughts of happiness, to be dejected with sorrow, or to shudder at wrong.

It was not until man appeared upon the scene, with his advanced brain, that a being was placed upon the earth conscious of the existence of evil and of perpetual conflict in physical and mental nature. He was *compelled*, from the very nature of his organization and its relations with external nature, to taste "of the fruit of the tree of knowledge of good and evil." He had been formed the chief agent in progressive nature for the expression of *mind* through *matter*, and was the first to consider an effect or to seek a cause. He did not then know that mind as well as matter was subordinated to a law of progressive development, and, with his inexperience, fancied the world was made on a plan conceivable to himself and presided over by God and evil spirits. The physicist was not there to show him the impelling and resisting forces of nature, or that all this conflict arises from this cause; not there to say that 'all the phenomena of nature can be traced to the laws of matter;" and that the full explanation of good and evil is found in the impelling Force of Mind operating through the resistance of matter.

But in man, who, though ever presently subject to the conflict of mind with matter, a being was formed endowed with mental capacity to ameliorate, modify and improve adverse conditions. That is to say, a being appeared upon the earth having this Potential Power of the Intellectual Force in persistent activity, under all influences, physical and mental, under the excitation of which he can never find rest—never reach a period where, under its influence, Hope will not impel him *to the better.*

"If we contemplate the course of human development from the highest scientific point of view, we shall find that it consists *in educing*, more and more, the characteristic faculties of *humanity*, in comparison with those of *animality*, and especially with those which man has in common with the whole organic kingdom. It is in this philosophic sense that the *most eminent civilization* must be pronounced to be fully *accordant with nature*, since it is, in fact, only a more *marked* manifestation of the *chief* properties of our species, properties which, latent at first, can come into play only in that advanced state of social life for which they are exclusively destined. The whole system of biological philosophy indicates the *natural progression*. We have seen how, in the brute kingdom, the superiority of each race is determined by the degree of preponderance of the *animal* life over the *organic*. In like manner we see *that our social evolution is only the final term of a progression* which has continued from the simplest vegetables and most insignificant animals up through the higher reptiles to the birds and mamifers, and still on to the carnivorous animals and monkeys, the organic characte istics retiring and the animal prevailing, more and more, till the intellectual and moral tend toward the ascendancy *which can never be fully obtained* in the highest state of human perfection we can conceive of. This comparative estimate affords us the scientific view of human progression connected (as we see it is) with the whole course of animal advancement, of which it is itself the highest degree. The analysis of our social progress proves, indeed, that while the *radical* dispositions of our nature are necessarily *invariable*, the *highest* of them are in a continuous state of relative development, by which they rise to be preponderant powers of human existence, though the *inversion* of the primitive economy can never be absolutely complete."—*Comte's Positive Philosophy, pp. 115, 116.*

Discard from the mind all commonly received notions of a Creation and accept the evident truth that from the beginning Formation began, and under the impulse of the Intellectua' Force has gone on through material, physical and mental nature, and will go on forever. Accept, also, the evident truth, that the Intellectual Force has, so far, *on earth,* found its best expression in the emotions and intellect of man, where it has awakened a recognition of its nature, of its purpose, and of the character of the medium through which it operates in the development of itself. Where it has awakened a recognition of its pervading, advancing and directing power in the control of matter as a medium for mental development.

Such is the order of nature—material, animal, mental—all subordinated to the Intellectual Force in its progressive development. Reflecting upon this order, a recent writer (McCosh) observes:

"In proportion as the sciences have become subdivided and narrow d to particular facts, is there a desire waxing stronger among minds of la ge views to have the *light* which they have scattered collected into a *focus.* As the special sciences advance, the old question, which has been from the beginning, will anew and anew be started, 'What is the general meaning of the laws which reign throughout the visible world?'"

"It appears we are approaching the time when an answer may be given to the old question. As there is a certain *law of progress* in the development of the young animal to the day of its birth, so there seems to be some traces of parallelism to this in the order of creation—a p ogress in uterine life, and *a parallel march* in the womb of time from the beginning to the day when man was ushered into existence."

"It is evident," says Agassiz, "that there is a manifest progress in the succession of beings on the surface of the earth. This progress consists in an increasing similarity to the living *fauna,* and among the vertebrata, especially, in their increasing resemblance to man. There is nothing like parental descent connecting them. The fishes of the Palæozoic age are in no respect ancestors of the reptiles of the secondary age, nor does man descend from the mammals which preceded him in the tertiary age. The link by which they are connected is of a higher and *immaterial* nature; and their connection is to be sought in the view of the Creator himself, whose aim in forming the earth, in allowing it to undergo the successive changes which geology has pointed out, and in creating successively all the different types of animals which have passed away was *to introduce man* upon its surface. Man is the *end* toward which all the animal creation *has tended* from the first appearance of the first Palæozoic fishes.'' The language of Owen is more explicit. ''The recognition of an ideal exemplar in the vertebrated animals proves that the knowledge of such a being as man must have existed before man appeared; for the Divine Mind which planned the archetype *also foreknew all its modifications.* The archetype idea was manifested in the flesh long prior to the existence of those animal species that actually exemplify it. To what *natural laws* or *secondary causes* the orderly succession and progression of such organic phenomena may have been committed, we are as yet ignorant. But if, without derogation of the Divine Power, we may conceive of the existence of such ministers, and personify them by the term 'Nature,' we learn from the past history of our globe, *she has advanced with slow and stately steps*, guided by the archetypal light amid the wreck of worlds, from the first embodiment of the vertebrate idea under its old ichthyic vestment, until it became arrayed in the glorious garb of the human form.''

So far science concurs in the demonstration of the Intellectual Force But here it passes in greater fullness into man, and his *ego* interposes and checks the inquiry, '' Whence do I get the capacity, the intelligence, the power, to understand a Force—to think or reason about it, as it is displayed in progressive order of development in all departments of animated nature ?''

Egotism increases as the animal instincts predominate, and decreases as desire and intelligence elevate the mind, until we come to regard ourselves as only parts of an Infinite Whole. Possessing no more intelligence or mental power than the brute, the *ego* can only comprehend the animal ; but possessing it in the full measure of man's capacity, it will be readily conceived how truly it was said, '' I and my Father are *one*,'' and that the Intellectual Force, contemplating man from the beginning as the highest earthly link in the chain of progress, is the Force enlightening our own minds, *as it is imparted*, or as the Force pervades our being.

But as it comes through the dark medium of matter—as matter organized into animals has its imperfections—its diseases, within and without, its appetites and brutal propensities, the light is varied, or perverted, or depraved, according to the organization and its environment.

Nature, then, has been progressive from the beginning. From the molecules to the worlds of space ; from the *formation* of the rocks, the waters, the air, the earth to life. From the vegetable to the animal, and from the animal to man. From the beginning we also see the Impulsive Force, from the molecules to the vegetable and from the vegetable to man, and the Directing Force, beginning in instinct and developing into mind.

The obstacles, or elements, conflicting with this Force. are just as apparent. In the grand progression of nature Instinct had its opposite in matter, through the medium of which arises, in vegetable and animal organization, everything, physical and moral, we consider evil.

Let us consider more definitely that principle in organized life we name Instinct :

" With the inferior animals there is a certain squareness of adjustment, if we may so term it, between each desire and its correspondent gratification. The one is evenly met by the other, and there is a fullness and definiteness of enjoyment up to the capacity of enjoyment. Not so with Man, who, both from the vastness of his propensities and the vastness of his powers, feels himself chained and beset in a field too narrow for him. He alone labors under the discomfort of an incongruity between his circumstances and his powers, and *unless there be new circumstances* awaiting him in a more advanced state of being, he, the noblest of Nature's products here, would turn out to be the greatest of her failures.

" This, then, I take to be the proof of the Soul in Man, not that he has a mind—because, as you justly say, inferior animals have that, though in a lesser degree—but because he has the capacities to comprehend, as soon as he is capable of any abstract ideas whatsoever, the very truths not needed for self-conservation on earth, and therefore not given to yonder ox and opposum, namely, the nature of Deity—Soul—Hereafter. And in the recognition of these truths the Human Society that excels the society of beavers, bees and ants, by perpetual and progressive improvement on the notions inherited from its progenitors, rests its basis. Thus, in fact, this world is benefited for men by their belief in the next, while the society of brutes remains age after age the same. Neither the bee nor the beaver has, in all probability, improved since the Deluge."—*Chalmers' Bridgwater Treatise.*

Scientists say, Man was manifestly the *end* of physical organization, contemplated from the beginning. In an order of Nature which has progressed from death to life, from vegetable Instinct to Mind, what is to be the end of Man? We see clearly a mental Force in Nature universally diffused through all the atoms of matter and all their combinations; directing the formation of the worlds, the material elements of the earth, developing into sensation and persistently seeking higher expression in thought, reason and emotion. An Overruling Force of Nature which has been so far imparted

to the earth as to have brought physical order out of disorder and a mental power capable of reviewing its own works
and of co-operating in the advancement of its own expression. This life is not the end of progression!

Reducing matter to the extreme point of divisibility, we
approach the Immaterial; that is, we approach that which
appears immaterial to us. We get back to the atoms, or,
the invisible "ether," far as " glass can reach," and the infinite beyond we term the immaterial. Electricity, heat, light,
attraction, are material forces, evolved as we conceive from
the combinations of matter, having well defined offices in
the economy of nature. Each has its opposite, by which its
power is limited.

It is said that Intellect, as displayed on earth, is also a material Force—having power and resistance. But observe,
that its power formed the world—formed all organized life—
overrules and directs matter and its forces. It is unimpor-
tant, then, whether we consider mind material or immaterial.
We trace it back far as we can trace the divisibility of matter, and forward, in its diffusion and development, through
all grades of life to the Emotions and the Intellectual Power
of Man.

Organic progression has been the history of living beings
from the first appearance of life to man. Parallel with the
advancement of organic structure has been the development
of Instinct—of the Intellectual Force—grades and diversi-
ties of development having been exhibited in the vegetable,
the fish, the bird, the mammalia and in man, according to
organism and physical environment. In man we discover
all of the animal instincts of inferior orders, and something
more. Desire, with the directing Instinct, for food; the
sentiment of affection; providence for the future; the love
of dominion, are all found in lower animal life But, in
Man, all instinct in sympathy with his advanced organism
has progressed in development. No new influence was introduced but that, from the beginning, again enlarged. Memory became more tenacious of facts. Judgment, more rigidly
discriminating, developed into Reason, and from this Reflection was educed.

So far, these instincts might be regarded as necessary to
the conservation of the advanced organism and their effects, as confined to this state of existence, had they not
given rise to other and higher instincts—having no relation
to animality—no sympathy with "this body of death." But
they have awakened in the mind of man consciousness of

3

Mental Existence and the recognition that this mentality is
Spirit seeking to discover its Source and desiring and expect-
ing a life suited to its nature, and that *that* nature can only
find its perfect enjoyment in the love of Wisdom, of Moral
Purity—of the Beautiful and the Good—in infinite progression.

Let the light so shine that no cloud may rest upon the
mind in the recognition of its own nature, of its Source, of
its inspirations.

Emotion is the Great First Cause, imparted to matter according to organization and environment. We know no
more of this Cause than as it is displayed in Nature; but
here we know enough to satisfy the highest reason that this
Emotion has its Source in the Soul of the Universe; because
science recognizes it, in all structural organization, as impelling and progressive in the increase and diffusion of its
own development, from chemical attraction to animal desire
and instinct, and from these to the highest emotions, desires
and intelligence of man, in whom it acts with increased momentum as an emotional, impelling and informing principle.
It is manifestly not only a procreation of mind but *Mind itself*, exhibiting in all of its qualities and effects—its desires,
thought, reason, knowledge, all that we can comprehend as
constituting a Soul. We know, too, that it has steadily developed through all the orders of organic life to man, and
through him has evolved all that is beautiful in Art, useful
in Science, truthful in Philosophy and elevating in Religion;
and that, with increasing momentum, it persistently urges
mankind to higher intellectual and moral excellence, while it
prompts his aspirations, while it fires his hope, his faith, and
enlightens his reason, to anticipate a state of perfect and immortal happiness in a life to come.

"Hence our good is a thing honorable and venerable and divine
and lovely and symmetrical and called, somehow. happiness; but of
the things that are said by the many to be good, such as health and
beauty and strength and wealth and what are near to these, there is
not one altogether a good unless it meets with the use of it arising
from virtue. And happiness, he conceived, to exist not in human
things, but in divine and blessed. From whence he said that the
souls of Philosophers in reality were filled with things great and wonderful, and that after the dissolution of the body, they become hearth-
fellows with the gods, and go round with them, while surveying the
level plain of truth, since even during the perio1 of life, they had a
desire for His knowledge, and honored his pursuit above all; by
which, after they are purified and revivified, as it were, some eye of
the soul, that having been previously lost and blinded, is better to be
saved than ten thousand eyes, becomes able to reach the nature OF
ALL THAT IS RATIONAL. But on the other hand, men without minds
are likened to those who live under the earth, who have never seen

the brilliant light of the sun, but look upon some dim *shadows* **of the**
substances that are with us and conceive that they are clearly laying
hold of what exists. For as these, when they meet a return from
darkness and arrive at a clear light, reasonably condemn what appeared then and themselves likewise for having been deceived before;
so they who pass from the darkness in which they lived to things
that are truly divine and beautiful, will despise what was previously
viewed by them with wonder, and they will have a more violent desire for the contemplation of the last mentioned."—*Socrates, from the
Works of Plato.*

Emotion is the fountain of desire, the Inspiration of Intellect, and has found, in all ages and climes, in various degrees
of excellence, its highest medium of expression in the human mind. It is a principle as unceasing in activity as light
or heat or electricity, pervading all matter, and declaring its
true nature in every well-developed human mind.

"And such trust have we through Christ to God-ward. Not that
we are sufficient of ourselves to THINK ANYTHING as of ourselves;
but our sufficiency is of God."—*Paul.*

> "Such harmony is in immortal souls,
> But whilst this muddy vesture of decay
> Doth grossly close it in, we cannot hear it."

It is with us alway and every-where, imparted as physical
organization can receive it, but still so imparted as to move
man onward, willing or unwilling.

" In every experimental science there is a tendency toward perfection. In every human being there is a *wish* to ameliorate his own
condition. These two principles suffice, even when counteracted by
great public calamities and by bad institutions, to carry civilization
forward. No ordinary misfortune, no ordinary misgovernment,
will do so much to make a nation wretched, as the constant progress
of physical knowledge and the constant effort of every man to better
his condition, will do to make a nation prosperous."—*Macauley.*

Emotional Instinct is the Impelling and Directing Force
of Nature—

> "That changed through all and yet in all the same,
> Great in the earth as in the ethereal flame;
> Warms in the sun, refreshes in the breeze,
> Glows in the stars and blossoms in the trees;
> Lives through all life, extends through all extent,
> Spreads undivided, operates unspent."

To man it gave the inspiration of Hope and its thought of
the Better, reaching out to infinite bliss, illumined with the
mystic dreams of the Imagination.

> " And thou, O Hope, with eyes so fair,
> What was thy delighted measure?
> Still it whispered promised pleasure,
> And bade the lovely scenes at distance hail!
> Still would her touch the strain prolong,
> And from the rocks, the woods, the vale,

"She called on Echo still through all her song;
And where her sweetest theme she chose,
A soft responsive voice was heard at every close,
And Hope, enchanted smiled, and wav'd her golden hair."

And Hope, pleased with her wonderful creations, however varied, strengthened them with Faith, and many confidingly rest in their assurance of the Better. But Reflection, not satisfied with the pleasing visions of the Imagination, must have Knowledge, and Hope and Faith summoned Reason to their aid, when the Stone Book was opened, the elements analyzed, the laws of matter defined, and Reason brought to Hope and Faith the Knowledge, that Impelling and Directing all matter, is the Emotional Instinct, the Intellectual Force, expanding from the Monad to Man, in whom it awakens to a sense of its Infinite Source, to a sense of its "muddy vestment of decay," of its pure and unlimited desires, of its love of the Wise, the Beautiful and the Good, and of its Immortal Destiny.

Behold! the common pathway from the infinite *past* to the infinite *future,* for Science, Philosophy, Religion and Common Sense; for the learned and the unlearned, brilliantly illuminated by Hope, Faith and Knowledge, with a vista of expanding Wisdom and Love boundless as the unlimited aspirations of the human Soul, and then—

"Pray of the Spirit who lighted the flame,
That passion no more may its purity dim;
And, that sullied but little, or brightly the same,
You may give back the gem that you borrowed from *Him.*"

THE MORAL POWER OF MAN.

Name it as you may, "The Breath of God;" "The Divine Afflatus;" "Attraction and Repulsion;" "The Law of Selection;" Emotion, is the original and impelling principle of Nature. It enters, in degree, into every atom of matter, singly and in combination, informing all in accordance with the forms assumed under its influence.

To this Emotion thought will trace all the phenomena of Matter, and man will learn why "we are born and laugh," in the angelic smile that plays upon the face of infancy; in the rainbow hues of Hope; in the pleasing visions of the imagination; in the carol of the birds; in the good and beautiful in Nature; and in the perpetual increase and diffusion of the pervading influence.

Let there be here no departure from evident facts—no postulate not as certain as the axioms of science.

Emotion is the impelling motive of Desire. Desire is the inspiration of affection and aversion, of instinct and intellect. Trace these through all animated Nature, and it is true of all life and in our own consciences.

In the earliest period of life's history Desire was confined to the conservation and multiplication of vegetable species. Later it was confined to the conservation and multiplication of animal life.

In this gradual diffusion of the Emotional force through organized forms there has been something opposing. resisting, or thwarting its expression. The conflict is everywhere obvious, in the material elements, in vegetable and animal life.

Let us realize that we have outgrown the mental infancy of our race, when, in this resistance, this opposition to the good, the imagination fancied evil spirits, or contending deities.

Consider that this resistance, limitation or perversion of the Emotional force, results wholly from matter, the medium through which it operates, and that its expression is limited or varied by vegetable or animal organization and environment.

[Organization and the influences of environment have been largely explained in such works as "The Constitution of Man," "The Spirit of Laws," and by all that has been written upon vegetable and animal physiology.]

In all the vast period of the earth's duration, from the primitive rocks to man, with all its varied phenomena, there was no expression of a Moral Sense. The supreme law of Matter was limited to physical nature; was a physical law, recently defined as the "Law of Selection," contemplating, in its influence upon organized life, the "survival of the fittest;" a law that has since reigned, and is still supreme, largely, in the conduct of man.

But in man the Emotional force expanded, enlarged its expression. Consider if it imparted to him a new Sense, a a higher Sense than his animality. If the instinct in him is confined to the animal appetites, passions and propensities; if it aspires to nothing above the gratification of animal desire, then there is no law above his animality, and he is no more accountable for his actions to any power above him than the ox or the dog, and can do no wrong save in contravention of the social order of the country in which he lives.

But if he carries with him the consciousness of being moved by a thinking, judging, righteous, benevolent Spirit, that loves virtue and abhors vice ; that is perpetually urging him in the pursuit of whatever is true, useful and good ; suggesting to him that his mission, in the order of Nature, is not simply to eat, drink and die like a brute ; but to sacrifice the animal, if need be, for the true and the good ; and that lifts him up, when its beam of intelligence is unimpeded, or unperverted by animal desire, to a recognition of its sublime purity—then he is awakened to a sense of moral law ; then he finds a higher Arbiter in the highest utterance of the highest Power of Nature conceivable to man.

The qualities displayed by this Spirit through man, under its physical environment ; its devotion to the useful, the true and the beautiful ; the good it has accomplished and the good it contemplates, let us briefly review.

———

[To be completed and the work republished, if desired.]

CPSIA information can be obtained
at www.ICGtesting.com
Printed in the USA
LVHW022151211218
601373LV00015B/501/P